NEW YORK REVIEW BOOKS
CLASSICS

GOLD

RUMI, Molana, Jalāl ad-Dīn Mohammad Balkhy (1207–1273), was born in or near the city of Balkh, in present-day Afghanistan. His father, an Islamic theologian, instructed him in prayer and fasting rituals while encouraging his studies in literature, science, and theology. When he was eleven, Rumi and his family left Balkh ahead of Mongol invaders, beginning a decade-long journey across Central Asia that ended in present-day Turkey. Following in his father's footsteps, Rumi became Konya's most eminent preacher and theologian. In 1244, he left behind his prodigious career to befriend the mystic vagabond Shams of Tabriz, his guide into the heart of Sufism. Ignited by Shams's teachings and by their ecstatic, tumultuous friendship, Rumi found his poetic voice. Considered the greatest poet of the Persian language, Rumi's major works are the *Masnavi*, a six-volume collection of mystical teachings in rhyming couplets, and the *Divan-e Shams-e Tabrizi*, a collection of lyric poetry dedicated to his spiritual mentor. He died and was buried in Konya. Around 1318, the historian Aflaki wrote Rumi's biography, drawing from Rumi's letters, the writings of Rumi's father and son, Shams's lectures, and interviews with surviving companions, leaving us a plethora of information about the thirteenth-century sage.

HALEH LIZA GAFORI is a poet, translator, and musician born in New York City of Persian descent. Her poems have been published by Columbia University Press and Rattapallax. As a vocalist, she has performed at events such as David Byrne's *One Note* at Carnegie Hall and Bonnaroo. She teaches workshops on Rumi's poetry at universities and festivals across the country.

GOLD

RUMI

Translated from the Farsi by
HALEH LIZA GAFORI

NEW YORK REVIEW BOOKS

New York

THIS IS A NEW YORK REVIEW BOOK
PUBLISHED BY THE NEW YORK REVIEW OF BOOKS
435 Hudson Street, New York, NY 10014
www.nyrb.com

The translator would particularly like to thank Dr. Marzie T. Nejad, who served
as a consultant on the Farsi text.

Library of Congress Cataloging-in-Publication Data
Names: Jalāl al-Dīn Rūmī, Maulana, 1207–1273 author. | Gafori, Haleh Liza,
    translator.
Title: Gold: poems / by Rumi; translations by Haleh Liza Gafori.
Other titles: Dīvān-i Shams-i Tabrīzī. Selections. English
Description: New York Review Books: New York Review Books, [2022] | Series:
    New York Review Books classics
Identifiers: LCCN 2020016145 (print) | LCCN 2020016146 (ebook) |
    ISBN 9781681375335 (paperback) | ISBN 9781681375342 (ebook)
Classification: LCC PK6481.D6 E5 2020 (print) | LCC PK6481.D6 (ebook) |
    DDC 891/.5511—dc23
LC record available at https://lccn.loc.gov/2020016145
LC ebook record available at https://lccn.loc.gov/2020016146

ISBN 978-1-68137-533-5
Available as an electronic book; ISBN 978-1-68137-534-2

Printed in the United States of America on acid-free paper.
10 9 8 7 6 5 4 3 2 1

CONTENTS

INTRODUCTION

RUMI WAS a preacher before he was a poet. Born into a line of Islamic theologians, he was a celebrity delivering sermons to hordes of followers by the time he was thirty-eight. Eloquent and magnetic, dressed in a crown turban and silk robe, he evangelized in mosques and theological institutions throughout Konya. Disciples and admirers from Nishapur to Damascus to Mecca called him Molana—our Master.

He was growing weary of fame. It was a trap, he would later suggest in his writings, as was dogma, as were the obsessions with title, rank, and prestige that plagued the religious and scholarly milieu. While touting self-transcendence, sheikhs and scholars pined for robes of honor and, as size indicated status, some stuffed their turbans with rags. Rumi longed for release from this stifling world, for a friend and seer unfettered by its concerns, for honest and intimate conversation. He hungered to actually feel what he called for in sermons: liberation from the cramped shell of self, union with a shoreless Love, with God.

This was when Rumi encountered Shams, a scruffy vagabond and rebel in a coarse felt robe, twenty-two years his elder. Shams was a free thinker, an independent scholar, and a well-versed mystic who worked as a hired hand. Content to remain on the fringes of spiritual and scholarly circles, he occasionally chimed in at gatherings or engaged in private discussions. He had a sharp tongue, an unabashed love for music, and a talent for piercing through artifice. Some dismissed him as rude and blasphemous. Others found his honesty refreshing and sought him as a sheikh. But Shams had no interest in followers. He wrote, "They kept insisting, take us as your disciples, give us robes! When I fled, they followed me to the inn. They offered gifts but I wasn't interested and left." Moving from town to town whenever he felt the urge, Shams earned himself the nickname "Parandeh"—bird.

Just as Rumi was wearying of celebrity, Shams was growing tired of solitude. "I was bored with myself," he said. "I wanted to find someone who shared my level of devotion . . . I wanted someone with a deep thirst . . ." It was providence, Shams would claim, that led him to travel to Konya and search for Rumi, of whose intelligence, eloquence, devotion, and talent he had heard. The two men met on an afternoon in November 1244 in a crowded bazaar. They had hardly stopped talking when Rumi descended from his mule and, leaving his entourage and social conventions behind, walked off with the dervish, his "doorway to the sun." The meeting was no less meaningful for Shams, who said, "I had become a stagnant pool . . . Molana's spirit stirred mine and the waters began to pour forth . . . joyously and fruitfully."

Shams set Rumi an array of challenges. He demanded that Rumi put all books aside and quit reciting passages from scripture, literature, and folktales. "Where's your own voice? Answer me in your own voice!" Shams insisted. On one occasion, Shams ordered Rumi to buy a jug of wine, which good Muslims were expected to shun, and carry it home in plain sight. If Rumi was to be liberated from the shackles of convention, he needed to let go of his good name.

Shams also introduced Rumi to the practice of *sama*, or deep listening. Conventionally understood, *sama* referred to the practice of listening to a book read aloud with the goal not only of acquiring knowledge but also of strengthening concentration. The successful student would receive a certificate called the *ijazateh sama*. Shams understood *sama* in a radically different sense. For him the object of attention was not scholarly texts but music and poetry, which he saw as a means of arriving at mystical trance, revelation, ecstasy, and divine intoxication. Shams and Rumi kept company with musicians and spent countless hours listening to music. It was an act of defiance to conservative religious authorities, for whom music, apart from singing passages from the Koran, was at best a distraction and at worst a sin.

Sama also came to mean the whirling dance, a demanding and joyous devotional practice to which Shams introduced Rumi. In *sama*, the dancer whirls counterclockwise around the axis of the left leg, turning forever toward the heart. With arms extended, the right palm turned up to the sky and the left down to the ground, the dancer becomes a conduit between heaven and earth, engaging in a 360-degree embrace of creation. As Rumi would say, "*Sama* is the food of lovers... In *sama* the dream of union is realized... The roof of the seventh heaven is high. *Sama*'s ladder reaches far beyond it."

Over the course of two years, Shams broke Rumi open. When outraged former disciples succeeded in driving the dervish from town, Rumi was devastated. This was when he composed his first poems, love letters to the absent Shams, who, on receiving them, returned. From that point on, Rumi would compose poems, while sometimes whirling to drums as friends wrote down his words. The sober preacher had become an ecstatic poet.

Rumi wrote some sixty-five thousand verses, which are collected in two books: the *Masnavi*, a didactive and narrative poem in rhyming couplets, uncovering "the roots of the roots of the roots of religion," as Rumi described it; and the *Divan-e Shams-e Tabrizi*, a vast gathering of lyric quatrains and ghazals. Here Rumi speaks as humble seeker, demanding sage, kind elder, and ravaged, ecstatic lover. With one exception, the *Divan-e Shams-e Tabrizi* is the source of the poems in *Gold*.

The ghazal is a sumptuous and demanding form, consisting of a string of five or more couplets, each one closing with a single refrain, or less commonly, with a single rhyme. Though linked by repetition, the couplets stand as discrete units, and their tone, imagery, and perspective are meant to vary and astonish. The word *ghazal*, the *Oxford English Dictionary* tells us, is etymologically linked to *gazelle* and like a gazelle, the ghazal moves by leaps and bounds.

Because each couplet of a ghazal is complete in its own right, it has long been customary for reciters, singers, editors, and translators, whether Iranian or not, to pick and choose freely among them. In *Gold*, I have worked in this tradition. Some of the poems here present Rumi's text complete; others reproduce the couplets that I felt spoke most urgently and powerfully. In a few cases, I found a couplet or line so resonant, I singled it out to stand on its own.

The languages of Farsi and English possess quite different poetic resources and habits. In English, it is impossible to reproduce the rich interplay of sound and rhyme (internal as well as terminal) and the wordplay that characterize and even drive Rumi's poems. Meanwhile, the tropes, abstractions, and hyperbole that are so abundant in Persian poetry contrast with the spareness and concreteness characteristic of poetry in English, especially in the modern tradition. I have sought to honor the demands of contemporary American poetry and conjure its music while, I hope, carrying over the whirling movement and leaping progression of thought and imagery in Rumi's poetry.

Translation, especially of poetry, is always a form of interpretation. Sometimes Rumi's lines lend themselves to literal transcription. Elsewhere his meanings baffle even the most well-versed readers of Farsi. At *shab e shers*, Persian poetry nights, it is not uncommon to hear people arguing about one or more of Rumi's couplets, offering their different interpretations. Perhaps it is his elusiveness, his leaps and paradoxes, the challenges of them and the invitations they offer, that attract so many readers and translators to his text.

On occasion, I have tried to elucidate specific words or characters by filling in allusions that would be clear enough to Iranians but perhaps not to others. "Aloeswood" and its scent, the word "raw" and its Sufi connotations call for a succinct expansion of text. So does Mansur. Rumi mentions him, one of the most famous of Sufi saints, assuming the story of his life and death will be known to all. I've told the story, knowing that it won't be.

As to the selection, I have chosen poems that seem to me beautiful, meaningful, and central to Rumi's vision, poems that I felt I could successfully translate and that speak to our times. Some of the poems have not previously been translated into English; others that have, warranted a new look. Ghazal 2144 has been translated by both A. J. Arberry and Coleman Barks. Arberry translates the opening line as

> Whatever comes of the world's affairs,
> how does that affect your business?

Barks, whose translation is based on Arberry's, arrives at

> What happens in the world,
> what business is that of yours?

My translation reads:

> Whatever the ways of the world,
> what fruits do you bring?

Very different. The second part of the line reads "*Kaareh to koo? Baareh to koo?*" where the word *kaar* means work, action, or career, while *baar* means fruit, cargo, or harvest. Arberry, I suspect, has left out fruit in deference to the common expression "*kaar o baar*," meaning business. Rumi, however, uses the two words separately so it is clear he is not making use of that idiom. Read as a whole, the poem, with its sequence of apocalyptic visions, challenges readers or listeners to consider who they will be. What generosity and kindness can they muster in times of public or private crisis? The fruit is the essential thing, the gift; the business is the matter of cultivating it and offering it up.

Gold, the title of this book, is a word that recurs throughout Rumi's poetry. Rumi's gold is not the precious metal but a feeling-state arrived at through the alchemical process of burning through layers of self, greed, pettiness, calculation, doctrine—all of it. In sum, the prayer of Sufism is "teach me to love more deeply." Gold is the deepest love.

Rumi lived to the age of sixty-six. He didn't return to preaching, though he remained active in the community of Konya, helping to resolve conflicts between townspeople, offering guidance and solace, writing letters to royalty to help poor students and others in need. And of course, he continued to write poetry, his greatest service. He spent the last years of his life finishing the *Masnavi* and writing the quatrains and ghazals of the *Divan-e Shams-e Tabrizi*, and even on his deathbed he was composing poems. The final couplet of the ghazal typically introduces the poet's name, as a kind of signature. In all of his work, however, Rumi never includes his name. Either he invokes Shams or he simply calls for silence, *khamoosh*. He was, above all, a devotee of the mystical state of *beenaame*, selfless namelessness, and a believer that anything worth saying emerges from silence.

I hope Rumi's spirit lives on in these translations and that his love, wisdom, and devotion to liberation move you.

—HALEH LIZA GAFORI
October 2021

GOLD

Let Love,
the water of life,
flow through our veins.

Let a Love-drunk mirror
steeped in the wine of dawn
translate night.

You who pour the wine,

put the cup of oneness in my hand
and let me drink from it
until I can't imagine separation.

Love, you are the archer.
My mind is your prey.
Carry my heart
and make my existence your bullseye.

Why paint night over nightless day?

Every religion has Love
but Love has no religion.

Love is an ocean—
no borders, no shores.

Drown there and you won't lament it.
The drowned have no regrets.

Colorless, nameless, free—
that's what I am.

                When will I see myself as I am?

Put mystery in the middle.

                Where is the middle in the middle I am?

                And this silver-tongued stream in me—
                when will it grow still enough to know
                the streaming stillness I am?

The ocean I am drowned in the ocean I am—
shoreless, boundless, wonderful.

Don't look for me in this world or that world.
Both worlds are lost in the world I am—

a luminous void beyond profit and loss.
Wonder abounds beyond fear of loss
and lust for gain.

                My soul, you are my true eyes.

What are eyes in the invisible visible I am?

                Then what do I call you?
Silence.
Words can't name what I am.

Then praise the wordless speaker I am.
I raced through emptiness, footless like
     the moon.
Praise the footless runner I am!

Why are you running—to reach me?
Settle in the placeless place I am.
Settle in the nowhere everywhere I am.

The moment I saw Shams of Tabriz,
I saw the supreme sea, treasure,
and gold mine I am.

You shattered my cup.
You shattered my cage.

Light, feast, triumphant blessing,
friend, trickster, haven for my drunken heart,

you brought my spirit to a boil,
turned my grapes to wine.

You lit a fire to the fragrant wood
and body of song in me.

Watch the smoke rise.

Just the other day,
fire whispered to smoke,
"No stick of aloeswood shuns me.

From its gnarls and knots,
my flames unfurl a honeyed musk
of amber, fruit, and flower.

It profits in perishing.
It welcomes me, even thanks me.

At the doorway to emptiness,
all knots come loose."

Cheers, my flame-eating friend
and Love-slain victor.
We saw you rise from the dead.
We bow in awe.

Look at the earth and sky,
pawned to existence,
one blind, one blue.

Beyond them, emptiness—a gold mine.
Joy streams from it.
Why flee? Lose yourself to it.

Turn the hard soil
and break the clods open.
Seeds will sprout.

To stand elegant as a cypress,
to caress a face,
every seed must shed its coat.

Churning and burning in the fiery gut,
bread turns into soul and mind.
What isn't transformed by fire
is eaten up by envy.

Smelt the gold and silver
hiding in the rock.
Glimpse what can't be glimpsed.

Wherever the soul soared,
fire was there first.

Everything I don't know,
Love will tell you.

Your laughter turns the world to paradise.
It tears through me like fire.
It teaches me.

Reborn in emptiness,
I emerge laughing,
here to learn from Love
new depths of laughter.

I've been short on courage,
but I have a heart of sunlight,
straight from the king's hand.
I stir up laughter even in those who fear joy.

Crack open my shell. Steal the pearl.
I'll still be laughing.
It's the rookies who laugh only when they win.

Last night, the spirit of dawn came to my room
and gave me a lesson in laughter.
Our blazing roars lit the morning sky.

When I brood like a rain cloud,
laughter flashes through me.
It's the habit of lightning to laugh through a storm.

Look at the furnace. Look at the stones.
See the glowing red veins?
Gold—laughing in fire, daring you,

"Prove you're no fake!
Laugh even when you lose."

We're fodder for death so learn to laugh
from the angel of death.
He laughs at the jeweled belts and crowns of kings—
all that splendor's just on loan.

Treetop blossoms erupt in laughter.
Petals rain down.

Laugh like the bud of a flower,
hugging the ground.
Its hidden smile opens to a laugh that lasts a lifetime.

Don't think!
Quit pouring thoughts like kerosene,
on everything fresh and green,
burning it to the root.

Be a fool! Drunk on Love, soaked in awe
till dry reeds are sweet as sugarcane.

A lion leaps out of his cage.
A man leaps out of his mind.
Bravery is delicious madness,

not some circumspect, cagey thought,
sly and ungiving.

Why scheme for a morsel?

Curb your insatiable hunger
and you won't be seduced by a trickster
or reduced to being one.

When greed groans,
I act deaf.

Who am I? Who is this I,
prey to so many temptations,
dragged this way and that,

drawn to the ear like the string of a bow,
shot forth like an arrow?

The moment I close the door,
an order from destiny falls on my roof.

Am I a star in the zodiac,
cycling through houses of fortune and disaster,
laughing in one, weeping in another?

One moment, I speed like wind,
the next, I'm a loafer.

One moment, I'm fire,
the next, a flash flood.

Now I'm levitating over the plains,
now I'm plodding through deserts and towns.

Where do I come from?
What rung do I stand on?
In what market am I for sale?

One moment, I feel the sorrow of separation.
One moment, I'm a mystery in Mystery's arms.

Now waxing and waning, in pace with the moon.
Now whirling and staggering, drunk on the divine.

Now I'm Joseph, thrown in the well.
Now I'm his brother, looking down from the rim.

One moment, bandit and ghoul,
one moment, restless and glum,
one moment, perched on a high roof.

Play the song mad lovers sing.
Let me hear their passion—
I broke through my chains.
I wrenched the post from the ground!

Stay by my side, beloved. Hear me out.
Don't empty this cup of compassion.

You are first and last,
the light and prize at this feast.

Pour wine from the tavern
where meaning is on tap.
For the devoted servant, there is no other wine.

In a field of logic, my words are horses
with no room to run.
Without reason, the voice of my soul soars.

Open your eyes to the four streams
flowing through you—
water, milk, honey, wine.

Pay no attention to what gossips say.

They call the wide-eyed flower jasmine.
They call the wide-eyed flower a thorn.
The wide-eyed flower doesn't care what they call it.
I adore that freedom. I bow to it.

Some say you worship fire.
Some say you follow scripture.
What do they know?
Labels blind and tear us apart.

Your eyes are not a vulture's beak.

See through the Beloved's eyes.
See one when your mind says two.
The angels adore your Love-drunk eyes.

Open them
and dismiss the vicious judge
from the post you gave him.

Bow to a human
and greet the angel.

Let's love each other,
let's cherish each other, my friend,
before we lose each other.

You'll long for me when I'm gone.
You'll make a truce with me.
So why put me on trial while I'm alive?

Why adore the dead but battle the living?

You'll kiss the headstone of my grave.
Look, I'm lying here still as a corpse,
dead as a stone. Kiss my face instead!

Salt dry land
blooms with tulips,
when you appear.

Sour grapes sweeten,
hungry for your lips.

Last night in my dreams,
I read your book of Love.
One chapter in, I was in ecstasy.
Your revelations are wine.

Your revelations are honey.
We are cakes in a row, waiting for your touch.
Sweeten any one of us
and our whole torn world tastes sweet.

Your face is the sun.
Our bodies are grapes.
Sweeten us with your light.

"Catch hold of the thread's hidden end," you said.
"Unspool yourself from self.
It's easy.

There are treasures within you.
Split the melon. Hand them out.

Have you seen Love's field,
the dancing heads, the blazing hearts?"

Lovesick, I went to the doctor of two worlds.
He filled a vial with my blood.
It beat like my heart.

Dear Shams, pride of Tabriz,
only you reveal the wound,
the root, and the cure.

I'm not that lion battling an enemy.
Confronting myself keeps me busy enough.

I am the soil Love seeds.
Roses and lilies bloom from this mud.

I ached from separation.
I cloaked myself in night,
emerged a shining moon.

Consumed in Love's fire,
I slip through any opening.
I rise like smoke.

I am a child. Love is my teacher,
waking me from ignorance.

Like Love, I will live on,
radiant, eternal,
when eating and sleeping are done.

Till then, like Bubakr, the master musician,
I quiet my mind and listen. I fast.

In silence,
we hear body become spirit.

You, leading the caravan, look at your camels,
head to tail, all of them, drunk.
The king is drunk. The captain is drunk.
Friends and strangers, they're all drunk.

Gardener, listen.
Thunder beats a drum. Clouds pour the wine.
The garden is drunk, the meadow is drunk,
the buds and thorns are drunk.

Whirling sky, watch how the elements whirl.
Water is drunk, air is drunk, earth is drunk, fire is drunk.

Don't even ask about the unseen.
Spirit is drunk, intellect is drunk, imagination is drunk.
And the mysteries of eternity—
they're the drunkest of all.

Liberate yourself from the tyranny of self.
Be humble as soil and you will see
every particle of soil is drunk on Love—
by the Creator's design.

In winter, the garden is still drunk.
The roots of trees secretly sip wine.

You have a jug of Love's wine.
Pour for all, in equal measure.
There's been enough brawling.
Friends, enemies, admit it or deny it—
they're all drunk, all whirling at the core.

Keep pouring. Loosen the knots.
Only a head steeped in the wine of Love
will tear off the turban and crown.

Pour the reddest wine for the ill and ailing.
Let their sallow faces flush with fire.
Let them burn with Love.

God's wine is light and delicate.
You can drink countless jugs.

Shams of Tabriz, in your presence, no one is sober.
Infidel and believer, ascetic and winemaker,
they're all drunk on Love, whirling through and through.

We exited the battleground and crooked valley of thorns,
we shed our twisted delusions,
and from a heartrending world of deception,
broke free.

Greed stripped everyone bare.
We knew its tricks, had played them ourselves.
We broke into the store of greed
and burned it to the ground.

Ocean waves roared at our heels.
We escaped just in time
and lay down to rest in a garden
where good luck seeds the soil.

We ride without horses.
We soar without wine.
No need for a jug or cup
and no debts to the wine seller.

We spun round and round,
making and breaking promises
again and again.

Under the eyelash of a new moon,
we leapt off the wheel
and landed on our feet.

We practiced for forty days, again and again.
We reached new depths of Love.
We realized the one we seek
is always where we are.

We listened in silence.

Love speaks in silence,
not in the rote words of schools
or the cries of the marketplace.

Gold gathers in silence.

No more words.
Rising sun, you release us
from the guards, the thieves,
the nights within us and without.

Where the water of life flows,
no illness remains.

In the garden of union,
no thorn remains.

They say there's a door
between one heart and another.

How can there be a door
where no wall remains?

Whatever the ways of the world,

what fruits do you bring?

Say famine strikes—
no bread or bowl of rice in the land.
Royal in rank, royal heart,

where is your hand?
Where is your measuring cup
and storehouse of grain?

Say earth and sky fall to idolatry—
all of us on our knees,
worshipping figurines.

Where is the idol
noble and clever enough
to break the spell?

Say scorpions, thorns, and snakes overrun the world.
Even so,
you're brimming with joy.

Where is your garden?
Take us to the flowers.

Misers rule. Generosity fades from memory.
Still, your eyes see. Your heart is full.

What wage will you pay?
What clothes will you offer the stripped and bare?

Sun and moon go down in hell's flames.

What light will you shine,
what fire will you light
before we can't see, before we can't hear?

No mouth to utter Love's secrets—

where are the silent translations
surging from your heart?

Dear friend,
imagine you're a jeweler.
You have more wealth than you can count.

What else would you do
but rain down pearls?

Come. Let's put this all aside.
We're drunk on a lofty ale and it's getting late.

Where, my friend, is your tavern?
Take us there.

Friend, cave,
Love that burns through me and consumes me,
you are the friend of my soul,
lift me up.

You are spirit, savior, slayer, and slain.
Inside your heart, mysteries stand naked.
Press my ear to your chest.

You are light, revelry,
the road to triumph,
the bird from the holy mountain.
I am the seed in your beak.

Drop and sea,
sugar and poison,
tenderness and rage,

room flooded with sunlight,
house of the wandering star,
garden of buds about to bloom—

you are all of them, dear friend.
Let me in.

You are day and night, the feast and the fast.
You are the harvest of my prayers
when I have nothing but hunger
for nothing but grace,
down on my knees.

Water and jug, soak me in your grace.
Trap and bait, cup and wine, raw and cooked—
don't let me be callow. Don't let me be petty. Don't leave me raw.
Cook me. Burn me up. I'll rise.

Restless with longing,
my mind and body weave web after web.
My own heart's ensnared.

When they trust, they stop.
The path to you opens without a word.

How could I have known this longing would drive me mad,
light a roaring hellfire in my heart,
make a river gush from my eyes?

How could I have known a flood would snatch me up
and toss me like a ship in a sea of blood?

How could I have known a monstrous wave would rise up,
crack the hull, fling the planks in the air, and drag me down
to the ocean floor?

How could I have known a whale would rear its head,
gulp down the sea, and leave a desert behind?

How could I have known the desert's cracked seams
would gape like a mouth,
sucking the whale down into bottomless depths?

Turn after turn.
Now there's no trace of whale, desert, sea, me.

How can I ask how?
Every how drowned in an ocean of no how.
Every what and why dissolved like salt
on my lost tongue.

Like every creed and school of thought,
I was awestruck, struck dumb
by the ocean's opium,
by the Beloved

flooding tangled groves of thought
with light.

What can I do but praise?

Ocean of hidden pearls, black sea of stars,
flowering fields of wide-eyed narcissus—
I exhale. You expand.

Shams comes from Tabriz
with the key and the practice.
Bitter turns sweet. We're so flushed with fire,
we open like a rose.

Here, it's spring, my friends.
Let's make our home in the cypress grove
and wake our sleepy destiny
till it surges skyward like these trees—

aliens rising out of the grass.
Just like them,
we are bound to the ground heading to groundless ground
where the soul flows,
nameless and free.

Here, let's take our bound souls there.

New leaf, you burst through the bark.
Tell us how to break out of our cage.

Cypress tree, you tunneled through darkness blind
and blasted through the soil.
What map was in your mind?
Tell me. I'll follow.

A flower steps out of its tight bud,
gives its nectar, gives its gold.
How do we do the same?

Soft white stars of jasmine,
sweet, dizzying musk of jasmine,
where is your garden?
I'll serve at the gate.

Dear nightingale, I bow to your bright songs,
never the same twice.
Master of improvisation perched in a tree,
flowers delight you. You delight us.
How do we pass on the favor?

Cypress tree, like a prophet dressed in green,
you whisper secrets from that alien sea.
Drawing down its pearls and coral,
adorning our ears.

Listen, you say. Listen to the flowers.
Listen to the nightingale
translating secrets into song.

Turtledoves coo at the moon.
Parrots sweeten our chatter.

The soul drinks their music,
wet and fresh as spring.

Ferment like wine
in the barrel of your body.

I saw myself sharp as a thorn.
I fled to the softness of petals.

I saw myself sour as vinegar.
I mixed myself with sugar.

An aching eye seeing through pain,
a stewing pot of poison,
I was both.

Reaching for the antidote,
I touched compassion.
I touched mercy.

I was a cup holding only dregs.
I poured in the water of life.

Raw and callow,
I followed the ones already cooked by Love's fire.

In the dirt on Love's path,
I found the medicine that ensouls sight.

Armor thinned to a silken scrim,
I sifted the soil that gives vision to the blind.

Love said, "Yes, you've arrived
but don't think it's your doing.

I'm wind. You're fire.
I stoke your flames."

Sun and moon of mine, you've come.
My sight, my hearing, you've come.
Ecstasy, you've come.
Eyes filled with sun,
harvest of all my longing, you've come.
Desert bandit,
penance breaker,
silver moon beloved, you've come.

Lantern in hand, I searched for you last night.
Today, you're on my path, a bouquet of flowers.

The moment you left me,
sweetness was stolen from my tongue.
I turned to wax, burned like a candle
all night, scorched by fire,
no honey.
No way to reach you,
no way to touch your beauty.

My body lies here in ruins.
My soul, a night owl.

The moon swooped down the dawn sky
and spotted me.
Like a falcon, it snatched me up
and whisked me across the sky.

I looked for myself, my hands, my feet,
saw nothing there.
Steeped in moonlight,
flesh and bone were invisible as soul.

Seeing only the moon,
I journeyed through mysteries,
to the highest of them all—eternity, eternal life.

Call it union. Call it shoreless light.
Sea of radiance flooding sight.

Nine spheres of heaven drowned there.
The ship of my being went down.

Reason burst back up,
bobbing through choppy waves,
babbling, boasting,
I saw this then that. I saw that then this.

The sea surged and foamed.
From every bubble, an image sprang,
a body took shape, marked by mind,
sentient, conscious,

rising from the sea for a spell—
a life—

before vanishing among the waves,
a flash.

How to soar with the moon
and drown in the sea?
Listen to Shams of Tabriz.
Shoreless light lives on his lips.

I'm not that unrequited lover, so bitter I flee Love.
There's no dagger in my hand,
no urge to dodge a challenge.

I am a wooden board the carpenter sizes up.
His ax, his nails—they don't worry me.

Let the carpenter make something of me.
If I resist, let Love's flames have me.

I'll be cramped and dark as a cave
if I flee the friend who finds me there.

I'll be frustrated, dull and barren as stone,
if I don't step out of my petty self,
take off its tight shoes,
and wade into rubies.

How many eons must pass
before the treasures I find here appear again.
Why ignore them now?

And why not seek my noblest self?
I'm not here to be ignoble.

I don't have a queasy stomach.
Why flee the tavern?

Why fear the prince?
I'm not a bandit, though I curb my heart.
"Quit it! Enough!" I tell it foolishly.

My heart answers back,
"I'm in a gold mine, deep in gold.
Why flee your chance to give?"

If you quit thinking for one hour,
what will happen?
If you plunge like a fish into Love's ocean,
what will happen?

When worries keep you up at night,
picture the seven sleepers
slumbering in a cave for centuries, resting in faith.
You'll be filled with holy light
no matter where you lay your head.

Straw man,
at the end of your straw world,
there's a fragrant field of amber.
If you leap from your high haystack and join us,
what new heights will you reach?

Again and again, you vowed to be humble as soil.
You broke your word every time.
When you keep it, what will bloom?

You are a gem covered in mud and clay.
Your beautiful face is hidden.

You came down from the heavens.
The high angel adores you and still,
you feel like a poor wretch.
If you remember who you are,
what will you become?

You seek truth but you don't trust
a single truth teller. I know a true seer.
Listen to him. See what happens.

A fragment, a hand longing for its body,
you dream of greatness,
grandiose fantasies,
gripped by greed, gripped by pride.

Give yourself up.
Give yourself over to glory.
See what happens.

You are a mountain full of gold.
Open the mine. Let the mountain speak.
Hear what happens.

Sufis arrive from the left and right,
wandering door to door,
alley to alley.

Where is the wine?

The heart is a door,
the soul, an alley,
and the wine flows from God's jug.

The cupbearer opens it,
calls out,

"Greetings, friends!
To drink this wine is not a sin.
To feel ecstasy is not a sin.

Feeling guilt for feeling pleasure—
that's your sin. That's your chain.
Shatter it, tear it off,

then invite the puritans over.
Today is an invitation to ecstasy.
Let them know.

If they turn away, let them go.
Let them judge. Let them talk.
Let them smear your good name.
You'll have less to guard!

Lover,
the eyes of lovers behold you.
Your friend is the sea."

You found me once again,
you thief of hearts. In drunken ecstasy,
you searched the bazaar and found me.

Even through sleepy-lidded, Love-drunk eyes,
you spotted me. I ran to the tavern.
You found me.

Why do I run when no one can escape you?
Why hide when you've found me a hundred times?

I thought I could lose you in a crowd of people.
But you find me even in crowds of secrets,
even behind my own masks.

What a blessing to be sought and found by your eyes.
What luck to be caught in your twists and turns—

loving seer, persistent seer,
towering cypress of countless gardens,

I was pulling a thorn from my foot
when you found me.

You showered me with flowers
from your fertile beds.
Dear nightingale,
your melodies opened my ears.

Like a ladle wanting its fill of light,
I plunged into the moon's halo.
At the bottom of that bottomless pot, you found me.

Like a deer fleeing a lion, I ran through the desert.
Deep in the mountains, you found me.

Wounded, I shed my blood on every path.
You followed the drops and found me.

I was a hooked fish writhing in the waves.
At the end of the line, you found me.

You roam the skies and catch galloping deer.
With all that skill and patience,
you found me.

The moment you found me,
you gave me a cup brimming with Love's wine,
heavy enough to match the weight on my soul.

Every sip lightened it.
Every sip, a balm.
I drank till empty.
My soul took flight.

I have no mind, no ear, no tongue today.
The source of thought and word found me.

Lovers, why fear disgrace?
Why should you feel ashamed?

Love is your unshakable kingdom.
Love is your throne. Your home.

A leopard, devoured by Love,
doesn't fear the world, its scents or colors.

A whale, hollowed out by Love's flames,
doesn't fear hell's waters.

Love's wine makes the cup forget it's a cup.
What will it do to a lover?

Pour some in a volcano's mouth.
Will it quit oozing fire?
Will it quit shooting stones?

You with a heart of glass,
learn from Love's sturdy cup.
If your soul is a trapped bird,
how will you fall in Love's trap?

Like a drop of mercury in the palm of a hand,
you wobble. Hold steady.

No need for me to speak
of the sea's transparency
when you can see clear to the bottom.

Grim and somber,
feeling guilt for simple pleasures—
joy is not a sin.

If you've made a habit of drinking vinegar,
don't blame the vine.

Ditch the vinegar
and ditch the vendor who doesn't deal in life's nectar.
Pour Love's wine and quit peddling misery.

Look at me. At this feast, I'm the lowest of the low.
I'm so far gone in ecstasy,
I can't tell up from down.

The spring of souls is here.
Fresh branch, budding branch,
come and dance.

And you, dear lion,
so fierce and hot-tempered,
come and dance.

You surrendered your head and feet.
Headless, footless, come and dance!

And you, rare king, true king,
nourishing as mother's milk,
come and dance.

A man arrived with sword in hand,
and venom on his tongue.
"Evil dwells here!" he said.
So does good, my friend. Come and dance.

Lovers whirl in devotion. Ecstasy, their crown.
Where they are, what use is the royal cloak?
Beautiful one, dressed to serve, come and dance.

You who are drunk on self—union is your destiny.
The map is in your hand.
Taste the rapture now. Come and dance.

If you're my Beloved bearing a cup of wine,
if you're a branch bearing no fruit,
come and dance.

The war is over. The band is singing.
Come and dance.

Unfurling its dazzling wings,
the peacock calls to the bird of the soul.
You without wing and feather, come and dance.

I went to the doctor of the soul.
"Look at me—I'm heartsick and in love,
sick and ecstatic, all at the same time.

I have hundreds of flaws.
One would be plenty.
I'm at my wit's end."

"Didn't you die?" the doctor asked.

"Yes, I died. Then you came near.
One whiff of your fragrance
and I jumped out of my grave."

Divine sunrise. Holy face.
He stepped toward me.

"Where do you belong? To what clan?" he asked.
"This one," I said.
I touched the hand that touched my heart.

I cried out in desperation.
He gave me a cup of Love's wine.
My pale face flushed with fire.
The battle was over.

I tore off my clothes.
Crazed, a student of ecstasy,
I joined the circle of drunkards.

I drank, spilled, shattered
cup after cup
till my blood fermented to wine.

There's a tribe that worships the golden calf.
I'd be a calf in the fangs of a wolf
if I didn't worship Love.

With a whisper,
the holy king summoned me to his side
and drew me up from the depths.

Soul of souls, I am yours.
Bow or arrow, I am in your hands.
Quick or slow, lucid or dim, I am yours.

You sent me whirling through this whirling sphere.
When you seal the jug, I seal my mouth.

Only your wine flows from my lips.

Full of yourself—
a friend's touch is sharp as a thorn.
A buzzing fly drives you mad.

Forget yourself
and what friend can hurt you?
You mingle with wild elephants
and enjoy the ride.

Caged in self,
you drown in anguish.
Storm clouds swallow the sun.
Your lover flees the scene.

Outside yourself,
the night is moonlit.
Lovers drink Love's wine.
It flows through you.

Self-conscious,
you're dry as autumn leaves.
You bite like frost.

Melt yourself,
and winter's frozen meadows
will become spring's fragrant fields.

Take the cotton
of the mind's doom-ridden chatter
out of your ears.

Hear the booming voice of the heavens,
the roar of fate,

the ruckus the muse makes.

Spring is here—
fragrant, musky spring is here.

The Beloved is here,
the Soul of souls is here,
the One who welcomes everyone is here.

Wine is here, the wine of dawn is here,
wine that floods the soul with joy is here.
The cupbearer fills everyone's cup.

Clarity is here—
stones in the river pulse with sunlight.

The cure is here, the cure for every ill is here.
The friend who soothes the ache is here.

The healer is here.
The healer who's felt every shade of feeling is here.

Dance is here, the whirling dance is here.
The eternal bond and glorious breeze are here.
Poppies, basil, and the tulips' stunning eyes are here.

One is here.
One who makes someone of no one is here.

The bright moon that clears the haze is here.
The heart stirring all hearts to laughter is here.

The Beloved is here, the Soul of souls is here—
and never left.
It's our eyes that come and go.

Be silent now. Let silence speak.
Surrender the syllables you count on your fingers.
The river of countless messages is here.

Why plague your heart with indecision?
Your heart is your pulpit and throne.
Don't step down.

Intelligence is your crown.
Only gems drawn from the depths of you
can adorn this crown.
Gather them.

When I am, I am not.
When I am not, I am.

You wake the dead to life,
you fountain of grace,
you fire in thickets of tangled thought.

Today you arrived beaming with laughter—
that swinging key that unlocks prison doors.

You are hope's beating heart.
You are a doorway to the sun.
You are the one I seek and the one who seeks me.
Beginning and end.

You greet need with generous hands.
You flood us with spirit,

rising from the heart,
lifting thought.

Rare one, you reveal the pleasure
of wisdom and practice.

Beyond these, what is there
but excuses and deceit?

We lust after the afterlife.
We stew over trinkets.
We stage battles between black and white.
Our ears are plugged with twisted delusions.

You carry the cure.

Silence!
I'm in a hurry. Leave the paper. Break the pen.
The cupbearer is here, jug in hand.

Meet us in the land of insight,
camped under ecstasy's flag.

Leave your tricks and schemes behind.
Go mad with Love.
Like a moth hungry for light,
dive into the blazing heart of the flame.

Be a stranger to yourself.
Wreck the house you call self.
Wake up in Love's house.
Live with lovers. Be a lover.

Why lie in a grave,
fearing judgment, hands idle?
You have a role at this feast.
Rise up. Open your arms, a haven.

Grudges and spite weigh on the heart.
Let seven streams of water wash them away.
Make room for Love's wine.
Be its cup.

Thoughts stray and drag you with them.
Heart, leap over your head.
Arrive before you know it.

You're not a rook bound to two directions.
You're not a pawn, a crooked queen,
a shortsighted king.

Be a mirror for your beloved.
Reflect what you adore.

Once mineral, then animal.
Now blessed with a soul,
be Love.

Preacher, how long will you rant
door to door, roof to roof.
Give your jaw a rest. Be silence.

The house overflows with drunkards.
More come knocking.

Crazed but still bound,
they tore off their chains.

You can't quiet this ruckus.
The heavens are beating the drums in celebration.

Ecstatic souls,
hearts that serve the heart,
broke free from their prisons.

They shattered the jugs.
No need for them.
Their bodies are barrels,
their blood is wine.

Oh God, what wine did they drink?
Oh God, what Love did they taste?

You're not a seeker?
Come with us.
Our curiosity is contagious.

Never played a melody?
Come with us.
Your voice will rise in song.

If you're hoarding vast riches,
walk penniless
through a land sown with Love.

If you're a master,
become a servant to the heart.

With a single candle,
we can light a hundred.

Living or dead,
you'll come alive with us.
We bloom with laughter.

Drop the royal cloak.
Dress in rags like us.
Feel the warmth of living hearts.

A seed must fall before a tree can rise.
Embrace this simple truth and fall with us.

Shams of Tabriz tells the bud inside the heart,
"The moment you open your eye,
you'll be a seer like us."

For forty years, my mind drowned me in thought.
When Love hooked me like a fish,
I leapt out of my mind.

See how the fruit is trapped—
first by its seed, then by its husk.

See how I was trapped—
first by circumspection, then by calculation.
Like a fig split open,
my seeds are bare.

Our first meal on earth begins with blood and ends with milk.
When my mind grew teeth, I craved more than milk.
I chased my daily bread
with a net, a mask, a bag of tricks.

When the Soul of souls caught me,
nourished me,
I shed my trickster's skin.

Silence! No more details—
I had enough of my own fever.
I leapt free.

Don't come without a drum.
We are celebrating.

Rise and beat the drum!
We have triumphed.

We are drunk
but not on crushed grapes.
Whatever the mind guesses,
we are far from that.

I don't know this nine-story house.
I don't know the nine spinning spheres
or the sculptor of spells
who set them in motion.

"Don't run off in so many directions,"
Mystery tells me. "Come this way."

I don't know that direction beyond direction.
And I don't know you either, dear Beloved.
Loving, jovial, sulky, cruel—
you always keep me guessing.

My soul wants to stir up joy.
My soul is restless without music.
But what is this merry soul? I don't know.

A hungry lion sees a herd of deer
and that's all it sees.
I don't know the lion or the deer.

A flood swept me away.
Now I long for a quiet stream.
Flood or stream, which will carry me home?
I don't know.

I am a lost child, roaming the marketplace,
wandering alleys.
Why the clamor? Why the secrets?
I don't know.

A friend warned me,
"People are gossiping about you.
Watch what you do."
Who's the critic? Who's the friend? I don't know.

Standing in a bakery,
I saw a loaf of bread rise like the moon.
I don't know the wheat, the scale,
the baker, or the moon.

The earth is a woman. The sky is her husband.
Like a feral cat, he snatches their children.
He devours them whole.
Who is this woman? Who is this man? I don't know.

A barren moon shines.
A sour world smiles.
What do I know but the light shining down?

You're ready for battle,
eager for chaos and blood
but too terrified to breathe a single breath
in awe and reverence?

Moment after moment,
a new being is born, rising like a tree.
Creation leaps from star to star.
Angels and demons marvel.

While pumped up and plump,
you fiddle with your mustache.
You boast of your manhood
and fancy yourself a lion,
fierce and domineering.

You're immersed in the unfathomable,
and you see nothing but yourself.
Be amazed.

Look how lucky the desert is,
a clear sky above and emptiness below.
Love travels end to end,
on every wind.

Come out, come close!
Why hide? Why deceive?

You are me and I am you.
Why get mired in me's and you's?

We are light upon light—
and the glass light passes through.

Why muddy ourselves with a grudge?

Together, we are whole and complete.
Why see through eyes that split one in two?

Why do the rich look down on the poor?
Why does the right hand scorn the left?
Both are from one body.
Why call one vile and one blessed?

One essence, one intelligence
thrust us into one curved cosmos.

Where the soul counts one,
the mind insists on two.

Five senses, six directions—drop the lot.
Leap forth. Let oneness
draw you closer and draw you in.

There you are a gold mine,
not just a nugget of gold.

There's one spirit in countless bodies,
one oil in countless almonds,
one meaning in countless words
uttered by countless tongues.

Shatter the jugs. The water is one.

Steeped in union, the heart remembers
a world beyond words.
Soul, send the news.

Your naked freedom
is your shield.

This time, I am wrapped and entwined in Love.
This time, I'm free of worry,
no thoughts of self-preservation.

Thought, sense, reason—
I scorched them to the ground.
I tore my heart out. I'm still alive.

Nothing ordinary here, my friends.
Even the Love-drunk ecstatic would be shocked to feel what I feel.
Even the madman spilling stars would flee this pitch of ecstasy.

I linked arms with death
and leapt into emptiness.

My mind second-guessed me,
chased me down,
tried to scare me out of surrender.

Why should I be afraid?
I give form to formless fear.
I write its every rant.

Once I lived in a prison of circumspection.
I thought I was being prudent and wise.
A prison. Why? What had I stolen?

I drowned in a sea of blood.
I wept like an untamed horse at bit and bridle.
I washed my blood-soaked clothes and mind in the soil.

Blood nourishes a baby in the womb.
Blood thunders in the baby's ears.
Reborn so many times,
I know that music.

Come into my invisible dwelling.
See through my eyes.

Love's wine flows here.
Drink with no mind
till you laugh with no mouth.

Music floats on wind
like driftwood on waves.

In the ocean depths,
pearls shine, lending their beauty
but never touching the surface.

We hear their dazzling echo.

Between the curtains of blood—
blooming gardens of Love.

Lovers gaze in awe.
The fruits of their labor—
beautiful, bountiful, a face of God.

Their work has just begun.

Reason scolds,
"There are six directions.
Six directions only! No other way through life."

Love laughs,
"There's another way.
I've traveled it countless times."

Reason saw one market,
opened a shop, and started haggling.
Love saw many.

The old mystic Mansur
trusted in God, Love, Truth. In its omnipresence.
Stepping down from the pulpit, he said,
Truth dwells in me.

Blasphemy! said the caliph. Hang him from a tree!
Unchained and in chains, Mansur danced his way there.
At the gallows, he rose.

Lovers drink dregs and brim with ecstasy.
Stone hearted men of reason seethe in denial.

Reason warns, "Forget union! Forget surrender.
The void is full of thorns."

Love replies, "The thorn is in you, my friend.
Constantly sounding the alarm. You call that existence?
Pluck the thorn from your heart.
Let the garden bloom."

Silence. My words are clouds.
Shams is the sun.
Let his rays reach you.

What else will a smiling bud do
but bloom in laughter?

What else will a flagpole do
but grip its wind-whipped flag?

If a ripe pomegranate on a branch
doesn't open its ruby mouth to the birds,
what else will it do?

Moonlight seduces you.
Sunlight feeds you.
What more would you want them to do?

When a shadow sees the sun's face, it bows.
When lovers catch a whiff of your fragrant shirt,
they tear off their own.

And the dead?
What else can they do but lie stone still?

Love, you strung my heart with gold.
What else can I do but sing?

Unless Love dyes you in its colors,
you're driftwood in God's eye.
You're stone.

Love unleashes water from every rock.
Love clears the rust from every mirror.

Blasphemy. Faith. War. Peace.
Love sets fire to all of them.

In the ocean of the heart,
Love opens its mouth like a whale
and swallows the divided world whole.

Love is a lion, pure and simple,
not a fox one moment and a leopard another.

Love nourishes and mends.
Love opens the clenched body,
lets the soul breathe.

Reason is baffled and spirit—
too dazzled to reason.

Divine wind,
my heart is in Tabriz.
Send my message of servitude
right away.

I was a dust mote.
Because of you, I am a mountain.

I lagged behind.
You urged me on till I forged ahead.

Because of you, I'm a cure for wounded hearts,
an ecstatic head,
a pair of clapping hands.

If wheat sprouts from my grave
and if you bake bread from it,
expect to get drunk.

The baker and the dough will lose their minds.
The oven will rattle off ecstatic verse.

If you make a pilgrimage to my grave
and stand on my burial mound,
expect to dance.

Don't visit my grave without a drum, my friend.
A feast with God is no place for sadness.

Asleep in my grave, mouth sewn shut,
I chew the Beloved's sweet opium.

If you tear off my shroud,
wrap it around you.
Open the tavern in your soul.

On every side,
drunkards brawl, drunkards sing.
One action breeds another.

God gave me life, gave me the wine of Love.
Death grinds me to dust
and I am still that Love.

I am the drunkenness born in the wine of Love.
Tell me, what is the wine of Love
but the ecstasy of loving?

To the heights of the soul of Shams of Tabriz,
my soul flies without delay.

I am blasphemous and religious,
the wine and its dregs,
an old sage, a young man, a child.

When I leave this world, don't say I died.

Say I was dead then came to life.
Say the Beloved whisked me away.

ACKNOWLEGMENTS

THANK you, creators of the Vajehyab dictionary, for gathering obscure and ancient meanings of Farsi words and offering them up. Thank you, Fran Quinn, for watching over the first sprouts; Zohra Saed, for that auspicious dinner in midtown; and Leonard Schwartz for leading the manuscript into the best of hands. Thank you to the wonderful team at New York Review Books, and Edwin Frank, for pushing me further, and for following the call of the cantos—evidence the work is working beyond the page. Matt Kilmer, next door and forever in my heart, thank you for your presence and support.

Deepest gratitude to my mother and father. This book is a testament to your love. Iraj Gafori, for the ghazals you sent galloping through the living room, long before I could glimpse their meanings. Marzie T. Nejad, for the countless hours you spent poring over the Farsi text with me. Always a blast, ride, and revelation to read with you. Thank you, Shams and Molana, for leaving us in awe.

INDEX OF POEMS

E XCERPTS or complete Ghazals (G) and Rubaiyat/Quatrains (R) numbered according to Foruzanfar's edition of the *Divan-e Shams-e Tabrizi,* unless otherwise indicated.

*The text of this ghazal is from Moshfegh's edition of the *Divan-e Shams-e Tabrizi*

TITLES IN SERIES

For a complete list of titles, visit www.nyrb.com.